UNSHAKABLE
LEADER

The Simple Yet Amazing Power of Alignment

John Opalewski

Unshakable Leader: The Simple Yet Amazing Power of Alignment
Copyright © 2020 by John Opalewski
Published by Converge Coaching, LLC
Washington, MI
Email: john@convergecoach.com
Website: www.convergecoach.com

Text & Cover Design: Keigh Cox

ISBN 978-0-9890546-5-2

PRAISE FOR
UNSHAKABLE LEADER

The title alone will get your attention—I certainly want to be an unshakable leader! The power of this book is John's wisdom gleaned from years of experience. John Opalewski is a leader's leader and a pastor's pastor. He will challenge you and inspire you to do the hard work required to be an unshakable leader.

Jenni Catron, Leadership Author and Founder of The 4Sight Group (Neenah, WI)

Experience often helps us understand that what we thought was cliché is in fact critical, life-giving wisdom. I suspect some leaders will read John's clear, intentionally approachable book on achieving a well-aligned life and be disappointed—pray, have good friends, practice emotional health, and maintain self-care. "C'mon John! Give me the wisdom!" He is! Experience will prove John right; it is these foundational, core, even "cliché" behaviors that bring life. If you see it as commonplace instead of wisdom, you probably just haven't experienced it yet. Buy the book, read it, and put it into practice.

JP Dorsey, President, Northpoint Bible College (Grand Rapids, MI)

Get ready to take a giant leap toward a more fulfilling and fruitful life. *Unshakable Leader* uncovers the master keys to enjoying greater influence, productivity, along with real joy, peace, and godly confidence. In this book, you'll discover the paramount leadership principles and practices that only a master-level leader like John Opalewski could impart. As you read *Unshakable Leader*, you'll quickly discover that John is not a common leadership coach. Not by a long shot. In his own words, his heart is to help you "lead better, lead longer, and have more fun along the way." I have personally met countless men and women who have experienced a fresh dimension of balance and alignment, excitement and adventure through John's coaching. Get ready for a transforming encounter as you read *Unshakable Leader!*

Dave Williams, Author, Art of Pacesetting Leadership (Lansing, MI)

This book provides valuable insights based on years of ministry leader coaching experience. The wisdom and insight gained from watching and learning from the successes and struggles of many leaders has been distilled into five critical leadership alignment concepts, all of which if understood and practiced can help every leader thrive and flourish under the heavy weight of shepherding and ministry responsibility. When a coach like John shares what he's learned, I want to stop, listen, and grow for my own personal benefit.

Hugh White, President, Full Strength Network (Mount Dora, FL)

There are many books written on the subject of leadership. In *Unshakable Leader*, John Opalewski cuts through the veneer of leadership achievement and performance straight to the leader's inner formation of health. This is a must-read in a time of mounting pressure and uncertainty. We need leaders who are responding from a place of health and vitality and John teaches us how to cultivate both so that as leaders we are ready to meet the challenge.

Michael Forney, Superintendent, Pacific Northwest Conference, Free Methodist Church (Seattle, WA)

John and the team at Converge Coaching have been successfully coming alongside leaders and pastors to teach them how to engage in healthy personal and professional alignment. I have been a recipient of that support in so many ways. The book, *Unshakable Leader* dives even deeper into this territory in a fresh way that will fully enable any leader to serve to the fullest.

Aaron Hlavin, Lead Pastor (Sterling Heights, MI)

CONTENTS

INTRODUCTION

UNSHAKABLE LEADER
THE SIMPLE YET AMAZING POWER OF ALIGNMENT

It's all about alignment.

So many leadership books have been written. So much great data to sift through. So many ways to "do leadership." But when everything is said and done (and read), it all comes down to *alignment*. The more aligned you are personally, the healthier you become. The healthier you get, the stronger the organization, family, or team you lead gets. Personal alignment starts with *you*.

Leading well is hard. My sense is in the days ahead, it will only get harder. Leadership possesses its great points, high moments, and victories. For a pastor, walking alongside people as they figure out their relationship with Jesus is fulfilling. Being invited into your parishioners' lives is an honor.

Leading well is hard

As a parent, watching your children flourish is rewarding. When they develop solid character, build great relationships, and discover their God-given destiny, life doesn't get much better. Watching them parent their own children well is a special treat.

In business, leaders love it when their team members perform at a high level, grow toward their full potential, and bring a winsome attitude along with them. Watching team leaders blossom before your eyes is exciting. Working shoulder-to-shoulder with high-capacity people is a blast.

But leadership also possesses a slimy underbelly. People are messy, and leading them often gets tricky. When an employee in the corporate world is underperforming, he is given a performance improvement plan, with a time deadline for making necessary changes. If after thirty-to-sixty days, no discernible improvement occurs, he is either reassigned to another role in the company, or let go. Personnel decisions like this happen every day in the corporate world. They are part of business culture, and nobody is particularly shocked when the hammer gets dropped. But it's never easy for a leader to make difficult personnel decisions.

Pulling off the same process in the church world is even more complex. Personnel changes happen, but they require a pastoral flair. Truth must be combined with love in pastoral settings. When a church staff member is reassigned or let go, churchgoers often are shocked because they see these kinds of decisions as unchristian or outside of their expectations. Often their response is colored by closeness to the particular person being reassigned or fired.

The increasing complexity of leading in the twenty-first century requires a commensurate increase of personal alignment in the life of a leader, or else he/she will find leading not only difficult, but dangerous. This could be dangerous to their mental and emotional health—threatening the health of the family, team, or organization they lead.

A landmark study of 14,000 lead pastors in the United States, conducted by The Barna Group, revealed 37% of lead pastors are at medium-to-high-risk of burnout.[1] Things aren't much better in the corporate world. According to Harvard Business Review,

25% of entrepreneurs felt moderately burned out, while 3% felt strongly burned out.[2]

Leadership health is central to a thriving team or organization. Our God-given mission and calling hang in the balance. *Unshakable Leader* is written for leaders who are healthy, and for those who are struggling. It's for those on a roll, and those feeling stuck in neutral, or perhaps even experiencing decline. It's written to help leaders lead better, lead longer—and have more fun along the way. The goal of this book is to encourage leaders who are healthy to stay well—and to assist leaders who aren't healthy to get well.

The journey toward leadership health starts with personal alignment. Achievement without alignment is possible, but problematic. If you get aligned in your personal life, it sets you up to win in your professional life . . . without success crushing you.

Let me give you a real-life parallel to illustrate the amazing power of alignment. I go to a chiropractor occasionally to help me address back/neck pain. My chiropractor let me in on a little secret: when he adjusts and aligns my spine, two huge benefits emerge:

1. My body gets more balanced and upright.

2. My central nervous system can efficiently facilitate communication between my brain and the rest of my body. When the spine is misaligned, my body is thrown off balance and is forced to work harder to compensate. The more aligned my spine, the healthier I get.

When aligned correctly in our personal lives, we're able to handle leadership challenges with more energy, effectiveness, and resiliency. When misaligned, success in our relationships, work, and in reaching goals seems harder and requires more effort. What's happening personally impacts us professionally.

Alignment isn't complicated. It's an unbelievably simple concept. However, the execution of it isn't always simple. Alignment takes practice, but it's so doable. It is easy to grasp the concept—and at the same time—so amazingly powerful.

Three Big Ideas

Throughout this book, the words *ownership, network*, and *rhythms* become almost mantra-like, because they are the overarching ideas or principles guiding us on the alignment journey.

Ownership: *You own the degree of alignment in your life, one hundred percent.* Your team is not responsible for your level of alignment or misalignment. Neither are your spouse or board. You, and you alone, are ultimately responsible for stewarding your personal alignment.

> You own the degree of alignment in your life

Network: Personal alignment requires a network of trusted people who speak into your life. A robust network includes your spouse (if married), a doctor, counselor, mentor, or coach, and some deep friendships to help you process life. Alignment rarely, if ever, develops in a vacuum.

Rhythms: Alignment isn't the same thing as balance. It includes an integrated set of rhythms which leaders develop—work/rest rhythms, physical rhythms, spiritual rhythms, etc.

Five Alignment Components

It's my belief the following five components are integral to personal alignment:

1. **Spiritual Hunger:** Maintaining regular times of meaningful connection with God. Encountering Him privately, as well as in public and small group gatherings, is foundational to personal alignment.

2. **Physical Fitness:** Integrating exercise, nutrition, and sleep to keep your body strong and healthy. Physical fitness has been undervalued in general by leaders. Our aim is to increase its value in your life.

3. **Psychological Integration:** Getting our thought processes aligned with truth, and identifying, owning, and processing our emotions. The way we think powerfully impacts our leadership influence and trajectory.

4. **Replenishing Relationships:** Intentionally carving out room in our calendars to spend time with replenishing and safe friends. Lone-wolf leaders set themselves up for trouble. Leaders who cultivate a network of life-giving relationships set themselves up for success.

5. **Life-Giving Rhythms:** Developing consistent rhythms of work and rest; solitude and community. Things in rhythm are healthy.

This book devotes a chapter to each of the five alignment

components. The following pages unpack a simple and practical pathway to their amazing power. The more aligned you are, the healthier you'll be. The healthier you are, the healthier the team or company or church or family you lead will be.

My sincere hope is the content found in these pages moves you toward becoming a more unshakable leader. The business you lead deserves it. The church you pastor needs it. The team you lead wants it. The family you parent craves it. *Bringing a better, less anxious, and more-aligned version of yourself to the people you lead is the most influential and catalytic behavior you bring to the table as a leader.* The impact will be deep, wide, and lasting.

So . . . it's all about alignment. Let's get started!

CHAPTER 1

ALIGNMENT COMPONENT 1: SPIRITUAL HUNGER

"Like newborn babies, crave spiritual milk, so that by it you may grow up in your salvation." ~ 1 Peter 2:2

If you're serious about getting aligned, a for-real, alive, relationship with Jesus Christ is the starting point. In Matthew 22:36-37 Jesus was asked: "Teacher, which is the greatest commandment in the Law? Jesus replied: 'Love the Lord your God with all your heart and with all your soul and with all your mind.'"

I surrendered control of my life to Jesus at age sixteen. I was a pot-smoking, beer-guzzling, foul-mouthed, angry teenager. Yet with the passing of every booze/pot party, I felt emptier on the inside. On several occasions, I remember staggering across the doorstep to my home and thinking, "there has to be more to life than this."

Enter my friend Kirk who lived across the street. I took interest in Kirk at age four because he had a red fire-engine big enough to sit in and pedal. I soon discovered there was something different about him. He was fun-loving, but it was the good, clean variety. I discovered years later Kirk loved going to church . . .

I as a young teenager, did not. After multiple invites to his church, I finally accepted. I didn't always understand what the people at his church said, but they seemed excited about Jesus.

On June 13, 1974, Kirk invited me to a Christian concert at a local coffeehouse. By this time, I knew what he was trying to do—get me "saved"—or in other words, convert me to Christ. I said yes grudgingly, but under my breath mumbled, "I'm not giving up the party life."

At the end of the concert, an invitation to follow Jesus was given. Despite all my plans to resist, I found myself frozen in time. I told Jesus, "Come be the boss of my life. I surrender control to You." Almost immediately, it seemed as though a load of bricks had dropped from my shoulders. For the first time in my life, I experienced a sensation of feeling clean on the inside. It felt like Jesus had power-washed me on the inside. My conversion was pretty dramatic.

> Possessing a for-real, growing hunger for relationship with Jesus Christ is foundational to personal alignment

Within twenty-four hours of my conversion, I had a Bible in my hands and a spiritual mentor in my life. His name was Rick. Rick showed me how to read Scripture. He taught me how to pray. He helped me learn how to share my conversion story. He invited me and a group of teenage guys into his life. He imprinted on us the daily discipline of connecting with God through the reading/studying of His word, and talking to Him through prayer and worship. What an amazing start to my spiritual journey! I wish every new believer in Jesus Christ would have a similar beginning.

Possessing a for-real-growing-hunger for relationship with

Jesus Christ is foundational to personal alignment. If you're out of sync here, the rest of the alignment journey proves exponentially more difficult. Health will continue to elude you. Working on our relationship with God over a sustained period of time helps us understand our identity is not what we *do* for God, our identity is our adoption *by* God. Leaders who lead from their identity rather than for their identity find it easier to stay aligned. But isn't it weird how our relationship with God can get squeezed out by our leadership responsibilities?

> Our identity is not what we *do* for God, our identity is our adoption *by* God

Psalm 63 gives us a great picture of what spiritual hunger looks like. Written by King David, this beautiful poem reveals his deep desire to be close to God both privately and publicly. Psalm 63 was probably penned while David was fleeing from Absalom, his son-turned-traitor.

Let's do a brief study of Psalm 63:1-8.

1. vv.1-4 reveal David's hunger for God. The entirety of his being—his soul, his body, his lips, his hands—yearned for communion with God.

   a) v.1: "O God, You are my God, earnestly I seek You; my soul thirsts for You, my body longs for You, in a dry and weary land where there is no water." The second word translated "God" in Hebrew is "El"; literally it means, "the Strong One." The Hebrew context here suggests David was feeling weak and exhausted. These words were a call from the depths of his being. They were a desperate, intense cry out to God.

b) v.2: "I have seen You in the sanctuary and beheld your power and your glory." David had wonderful experiences with God at the tabernacle, but now he found himself in the desert. Psalm 63 teaches us God's presence is not confined to any one place. It can be experienced wherever we are and enjoyed whenever our hearts long and thirst for Him.

c) v.3: "Because Your love is better than life, my lips will glorify You." David tells us that to walk closely with God is better than life at its best.

2. vv.5-8 reveals David remembering God

a) v.5: "My soul will be satisfied as with the richest of foods; with singing lips my mouth will praise You." This verse describes the fulfillment of David's spiritual appetite. Friends, I like thick, juicy steaks. But in the pursuit of God lives a depth of relationship with Him that is comparable to the best filet we can consume—only better!

b) v.6: "On my bed I remember You; I think of You through the watches of the night." David was on the run when he wrote this Psalm and apparently not sleeping well. A powerful truth revealed in verse six is how spiritual hunger is not limited to twenty minutes per day in the morning—or when life is easy. Opportunities to cultivate passion for God appear at unusual times and in unexpected places.

c) v.7: "Because You are my help, I sing in the shadow of Your wings." David's passion for God swelled as he remembered what God had done for him. I absolutely love verse eight:

d) V. 8: "My soul clings to You; Your right hand upholds me." Here we are given a glimpse into the depth of David's intimacy with God. The Hebrew word translated *"clings"* literally means *"glued."* David told his heavenly Father, "My soul is glued to You." Wow—don't you long for a relationship with Jesus like David's?

This psalm gives us a picture of what intense hunger for God looks like. The question is: Can we experience the same level of passion for God as King David had? If so, how do we get there? Let me try to unpack for you a pathway to developing spiritual hunger.

Spiritual hunger is not for a select few

In Isaiah 26:8-9, the prophet writes: "Yes, LORD, walking in the way of Your laws, we wait for You; Your name and renown are the desire of our hearts. My soul yearns for You in the night; in the morning my spirit longs for You." Listen to the verbs Isaiah used: "yearn" and "long." Is that level of spiritual hunger really possible for us? Or is it attainable only for "really spiritual" people like the prophet?

2 Chronicles 15:15 tells us: "All Judah rejoiced about the oath because they had sworn it wholeheartedly. They sought God eagerly, and he was found by them. So, the LORD gave them rest on every side." Spiritual passion is not for a select few. It's available to every leader.

Spiritual hunger flows from our habits

Do you drink coffee? Did you have to develop a taste for coffee? Do you now crave it in the morning? Do you need coffee right now? I hate to compare hunger for God with coffee, but the truth is we acquire a spiritual appetite over time and through repetition and soon it becomes as natural as our morning cup of joe.

> Spiritual hunger flows from our habits

Let's get practical: If you will read the Bible and pray up to four days per week, and do these behaviors four weeks in a row—even if it's only 15-20 minutes per session—you will build a habit and spiritual hunger will grow. Passion for God flows from our habits. The more we read, study, and meditate on His word, the more our appetite for Him grows. The more we pray, and worship, the hungrier we get. The less we read and study His word, pray, and worship, the less hungry we become.

In Psalm 27:8 David writes, "My heart says of You, "Seek his face!" Your face, LORD, I will seek." David understood a profound truth: *We can intentionally fuel spiritual passion.* And it can grow to a place where we don't debate with ourselves every morning, "Hmm, I wonder if I should read the Bible and pray this morning?" All debating ceases. Seeking God passionately becomes a natural part of our day.

You and I can intentionally cultivate hunger and thirst for God. We don't have to wait for a leadership conference, or hope to be "struck by spiritual lightning," whatever that is. Spiritual hunger is not for a select few. It flows from our habits.

Spiritual hunger grows when we share our story

Earlier in this chapter I introduced you to Rick, my first spiritual mentor. Rick helped me figure out how to tell the story of my conversion at age sixteen. What I didn't understand then is this: Telling our conversion story fuels spiritual hunger. In Psalm. 63:3 David said to His Heavenly Father, "Because Your love is better than life, my lips will glorify You."

Sharing our story ignites and reignites our spiritual passion. It brings us back to the moment of our conversion over and over again. Sharing our story is a constant reminder of how much we have been forgiven, of how empty our lives were before Christ and how full they have become after Christ. Verbally declaring God's goodness fuels spiritual passion. Unfortunately, leadership busyness often gets in the way of us telling others about what Jesus has done for and in our lives.

Hunger for God is contagious

In John 7:37-39 we read these words: "On the last and greatest day of the Feast, Jesus stood and said in a loud voice, 'If anyone is thirsty, let him come to Me and drink. Whoever believes in Me, as the Scripture has said, streams of living water will flow from within him.' By this He meant the Spirit, whom those who believed in Him were later to receive."

> A growing spiritual hunger cannot be self-contained

Streams of living water will flow out of us. Wow. In other words, growing spiritual hunger cannot be self-contained. It spills over onto those near us. Other people are positively impacted when you and I develop an intense spiritual appetite. Our family, our team, our church, and/or our business benefit greatly when we develop a hunger for Jesus.

Cultivating desire for the living God can be achieved in multiple ways. You'll have to find a rhythm that works best for you. But let me open up my walk with God to you here. Perhaps you'll pick up a helpful idea or two. Here's the bottom line:

Make room for meaningful times of connection with God every day

My first appointment every morning is with Father God. The break of day works best for me. Find the time which works best for you and stick with it. These daily connection times with God include worship, prayer, reading, studying Scripture, and often, journaling.

1. **Worship**

   I plug in my earbuds, hit the Spotify worship library, and spend time singing quietly to the Lord. Worship centers us. It helps us sense God's nearness. We tap into strength way beyond our own resources when starting our connection time with God by singing His praises. Worship sets the table for our conversation with Him.

2. **Prayer**

   I'm extremely structured when it comes to prayer. When praying for others, items like their walk with God, their relationships with people, their physical, emotional, and spiritual health are often part of my prayer assignment. I include special requests they mention as well. Here's the layout of my prayer week:

   Monday: Concentrated prayer for my wife, sons, daughters-in-law, and grandbabies.

   Tuesday: Focused prayer for our home church's pastoral staff, including their spouses and children.

   Wednesday: Spotlighted prayer for my family of origin.

I have eight siblings, so this prayer session is extended. I include their spouses, children, and grandchildren.

Thursday: Centered prayer for my wife Laura's family.

Friday: I zero in on prayer for a subset of my clients.

Saturday: Saturday is a change of pace in my prayer week. I grab my journal, sit quietly in a recliner, and imagine Jesus sitting in the chair next to me. I don't say anything . . . I just try to get quiet and listen for about twenty minutes. Sometimes I sense Jesus downloading thoughts to me—which I write down in a journal—other times I just sit quietly and enjoy His company.

Sunday: Brief prayer for all of my clients. I ask God to use them powerfully in their weekend gatherings, to do amazing things in the lives of the people they lead.

This may be too much structure for you. But if you have no structure at all in your prayer life, incorporating some routine, at least for a while, might prove extremely useful.

3. Word structure

I am a systematic reader of Scripture. I'm not a fan of hopping around when it comes to studying God's word. It's too easy to miss important truths. It's likely we'll read only what comforts us at the expense of what challenges us. It's more possible we will take verses of Scripture out of the grander context of the entire Bible.

We encourage all leaders to take a systematic approach in order to get a comprehensive view of God's revelation through His written word. The older I get, the less volume of Scripture I read . . . the more I ponder what's been read.

My Bible is overrun with notes in the margins. Here is where I capture thoughts and revelations occurring in the moment of reading a passage.

> It's likely we'll read only what comforts us at the expense of what challenges us

When it comes to connecting with God through His word, really think and pray about what you're studying, and how you can incorporate into your day the truths found therein. In Psalms 1:2-3 we read, "But his delight is in the law of the Lord, and on His law he meditates day and night. He is like a tree planted by streams of water, which yields its fruit in season and whose leaf does not wither. Whatever he does prospers."

My first spiritual mentor Rick impressed on me the importance of committing verses of the Bible to memory. It's difficult to explain how important this practice became. For example, Psalm 119:11 asserts: "I have hidden your word in my heart that I might not sin against you." Another verse I memorized was "The entrance of your word brings light" (Psalm 119:130).

4. Journaling

Journaling is a newer addition to my walk with God. I've been journaling for about ten years. I don't journal daily. I'm more of an on-demand journaling person. So probably two or three times each week, I actively journal—jotting down thoughts, impressions, and even questions that come to me during time alone with God.

You may be wondering why I've taken so much time to share my devotional life with you in this chapter. Here's why: If you don't incorporate the spiritual hunger component of alignment, the next four components are built on a

> If you lead without love for God, you've missed the point of leadership entirely

shaky foundation. Hunger for God is foundational to personal alignment. If you lead without love for God, you've missed the point of leadership entirely.

The following passage from the book of Revelation drives home the relationship between love for God and leading:

To the angel of the church in Ephesus write: These are the words of Him who holds the seven stars in His right hand and walks among the seven golden lampstands. I know your deeds, your hard work and your perseverance. I know that you cannot tolerate wicked men, that you have tested those who claim to be apostles but are not, and have found them false. You have persevered and endured hardships for My name, and have not grown weary. Yet I hold this against you: You have forsaken your first love. (Revelation 2:1-4)

The church of Ephesus was doing a lot of right things, but neglected the most important thing: love for God. The passage implies they still loved Jesus, but with a quality and intensity less than their initial love. We don't want to end up like these Ephesian believers. The only way to avoid it? Get serious about developing and maintaining spiritual hunger.

Bringing a spiritually hungrier version of yourself to the church, business, team, or family you lead will make an impact in a deep and meaningful way.

Let's review:

1. Spiritual passion is available to every leader.
2. It flows from our habits.
3. It grows when we share the story of our conversion with others.
4. It spills over its banks and positively impacts those around us.

Perhaps you're reading this chapter and feel unsure about your relationship with Jesus. Maybe you've never had a for-real walk with Him. Where do you start? Romans 10:9 gives us an idea: "That if you confess with your mouth 'Jesus is Lord,' and believe in your heart that God raised Him from the dead, you will be saved." You begin a relationship with Jesus by believing God raised Him from the dead, and by surrendering the right to be your own boss. That's it. A sincere prayer incorporating those two elements gets you started with a for-real relationship with Jesus Christ. And you are on your way to getting aligned personally.

But your alignment journey is just beginning. More work is to be done. In the next chapter, we'll explore the second component of alignment: physical fitness.

Reflection questions

1. Am I giving sufficient time and attention to the cultivation of my inner life? If not, what changes do I need to make?
2. Do I need more passion and hunger in my walk with God?
3. What am I willing to do about it starting today?

CHAPTER 2

ALIGNMENT COMPONENT 2: PHYSICAL FITNESS

"Take care of your body. It's the only place you have to live"
~ Jim Rohn[1]

Physical fitness and its impact on leadership often seem like the final frontier when it comes to personal alignment and health. When I talk to leaders about getting their bodies in shape, I'm often greeted with blank stares and awkward silence.

> We can serve God and others better when we're physically fit

Can I confess this component is an ongoing battle for me as well? It doesn't come easy; I have to work hard at staying fit.

1 Timothy 4:8 says, "For physical training is of some value, but godliness has value for all things, holding promise for both the present life and the life to come." Leaders tend to point at Paul's words here to the young pastor Timothy as their rationale for ignoring their bodies. Notice Paul didn't tell his youthful apprentice physical training was of no value. He stated it was of some value. Paul indicated physical fitness had a place in a

leader's life. I'll take it one step further—*we can serve God and others better when we're physically fit.*

What I'm about to outline in this chapter comes with two caveats upfront:

1. I'm not a medical doctor, a nutritionist, nor a fitness trainer. Adding these experts into your network is highly recommended.
2. If you're not currently in an exercise program, check with your medical doctor before getting started. Your doctor is an important part of your alignment journey. One of the first questions we ask clients who report suffering from burnout and/or depression is, "When was the last time you had a physical exam?"

Burnout and depression can potentially issue from hormonal imbalances. For example, people with low levels of the thyroid hormone often experience fatigue, weight gain, irritability, memory loss, and low mood. When the hormonal imbalance is treated, it usually reduces these symptoms of depression.

When it comes to physical fitness, I am thinking about three main categories: Exercise, nutrition, and sleep. Obviously more contributors to physical fitness exist than just these three—but exercise, nutrition, and sleep are huge factors in our well-being.

Exercise

Leadership can be sedentary. So we encourage leaders to get their bodies moving. Exercise brings both physiological and psychological benefits. Leaders don't have to be bodybuilders to benefit from exercise—they just need to put their bodies in motion. Some say I'm meddling when it comes to physical fitness and should butt out. I understand; it's a touchy subject.

When I mention exercise at leadership gatherings, I've yet to receive an "amen" or "attaboy." You would think after fifteen years, I would get at least one of those, right? I guess the silence speaks to this: taking care of our bodies is often the last thing on the mind of a CEO, a pastor, a parent, or a team leader. I want to move fitness up on your priority list.

> When it comes to exercise, consistency is king

When it comes to exercise, consistency is king. I get to the gym four days each week. I lift weights, and do cardio routines. When the weather cooperates, my wife Laura and I add walking outside to our exercise regimen.

Our goal is not to become body-builders; rather, it's to be body-movers. We try to keep our bodies in motion. I was taught as a teenager how to exercise by a personal trainer. The right breathing techniques, and the importance of proper form were imprinted early. So it's not how much weight you pump, or how fast you run . . . consistency, using proper form and technique, is what matters most.

You don't have to spend a fortune to get physically fit. Some gyms cost ten dollars per month and offer free personal trainers. If those aren't incentive enough to get your body moving, find a workout buddy who will hold you accountable. When I was a youth pastor, I used to lift weights with some of the guys from the youth group. One of the students used to call me regularly, and in a voice deeper than normal for a young guy, would ask, "Hey Conan, you wanna lift?" His timing always seemed to coincide with days I was thinking about skipping the gym. Just the other day, Laura asked me, "Do you want to go out for a walk?" I really didn't want to, but at her urging I reluctantly agreed. After the walk I thanked her for pushing me.

Some researchers disagree with the idea of a positive relationship between working out and emotional well-being. But for me personally, when I've had a stressful day, there is nothing like pounding the weights at the gym and getting outside for a walk to bring relief.

Exercise does much more than help us physically. It positively impacts our emotions. Exercise reduces stress, and releases feel-good chemicals in our brain. Some neuroscientists believe exercise even helps to create new brain cells. How many of you could use a few more of those? With the blessing of your physician, get your body moving. It helps you get and stay aligned.

Nutrition

You can't out-exercise a bad diet

A good friend told me several years ago, "John, you can't out-exercise a bad diet." Such great advice. What we put in our bodies (and how much of it) really makes a difference in getting fit. Most people know good nutrition plus physical activity can help maintain a healthy weight. But the benefits of good nutrition go way beyond what the scales tell us. Nutritious eating helps us:

1. Reduce the risk of some diseases, including heart disease, diabetes, stroke, some cancers, and osteoporosis
2. Reduce high blood pressure
3. Improve our ability to fight off illness
4. Improve our ability to recover from illness or injury
5. Increase our energy level

Good nutrition means your body gets the nutrients, vitamins, and minerals it needs to work at its best. If you need the help of a professional, type the word "nutritionist" into Google search and you will find a number of excellent options.

Of course, some nutritionists claim their eating plan is the only way or the best way to physical health. The truth is, many paths to good nutrition exist. After years of trying various ways to eat healthier, I've finally landed on a plan that works for me. My approach may not work for you. Find a nutritional strategy that helps you eat better, a pathway that is sustainable over your lifetime, while allowing you some flexibility. An occasional "cheat meal" can actually help you stay on track. It can jumpstart your metabolism, and help with insulin/hormone regulation.

Unfortunately, leading a business or a nonprofit doesn't naturally set up a leader for good nutrition. A leader's work hours are often weird. Their jobs usually don't fit neatly into a "9-to-5" box, and consequently, leaders tend to eat at unconventional times of the day. Because their schedules are often erratic, they often reach for convenience over health when eating. Fast food, comfort food, and binge eating are all too common for busy leaders.

Better nutrition lends to better alignment. The term "social-distancing" has become mainstream during the COVID-19 pandemic. It speaks to maintaining a six-foot distance from people to limit the spread of the virus. Someone recently said we should maintain social distance from our refrigerators to limit the spread of our waistline.

Sleep

The average adult requires six-eight hours of sleep per night to remain physically fit. I remember a colleague many years ago declaring: "Sleep is a disposable commodity." Those words might sound heroic to some, but in that moment, his words sounded plain stupid. They still do. "Sleep is a disposable commodity" might be one of the dumbest things ever spoken.

Sleep is a leader's cheat code.

> Sleep is a leader's cheat code

The better we sleep, the less issues we have with obesity or high blood pressure. Our brain actually repairs itself and flushes out toxins when we sleep. A pattern of good sleep makes us less susceptible to depression and/or anxiety. Chronic insomnia makes us five times more susceptible to depression. Great sleep enhances our mood. Our teammates enjoy being around us more when we're not sleep-deprived.

So it makes perfect sense: the more consistent our sleep, the better we can lead. Psalm 127:2 says, "In vain you rise up early and stay up late, toiling for food to eat—for He grants sleep to those He loves." These words were penned by King Solomon, perhaps the most accomplished king in all Israel's history. It's funny isn't it? Sleep was a priority for a king who accumulated more wealth than any king before or after him; who built beautiful buildings; whose wisdom was sought out by world leaders. "He grants sleep to those He loves." Doesn't it make sense to follow the lead of the wisest man (except Jesus) who ever lived when it comes to getting enough shut eye every night?

In the United States, busyness gets embraced far more often than proper sleep. A packed calendar is often viewed by leaders as a badge of honor. Unfortunately, those who follow these overcommitted leaders often applaud them for how "dedicated and selfless" they are. The applause often feeds even higher levels of activity in the leader, which is accompanied by even more applause. It's a vicious and dangerous cycle.

If you're leading a team, or a business, or a church, please hear me: *enough of the "I'll sleep when I die" bravado.* Let's stop being impressed by executives who consistently burn the midnight oil, skip sleep, and who wear weariness as an Olympic medal. According to King Solomon, God apparently is not impressed with those misbehaviors either. With all due respect, please quit playing Russian roulette with your physical health and get the proper amount of sleep. The negative effects of sleep deprivation are so great that people who are hungover from drinking too much alcohol outperform those lacking sleep.

Why should you care about sleep? One major reason is: God has called you to run a marathon, not a sprint. Sleep-deprived leaders cannot run the long-distance race they've been called to. Jimmy Dodd, in his book *Survive or Thrive*, asked John Stott, one of the most influential evangelical figures of the last century, the following question: "Dr. Stott, do you ever feel like just giving up on the Christian life?"

Stott responded: "Yes Jimmy, I often feel like giving up on the Christian life. But when I feel this way, I always do the same thing. First, I catch up on my sleep. I find that when I catch up on my sleep, those feelings almost always dissipate." Sleep is an irrefutably powerful force for good in the life of a leader.[2]

God has called you to run a marathon, not a sprint

Perhaps you buy in to the idea of proper hibernation each night, but you are struggling with insomnia. Once again, if sleep is elusive, reach out to your physician for help. Sometimes you have to consult with sleep professionals to experience better shut eye. Additionally, here are a few sleep hacks I've found extremely helpful. You have to figure out what works for you, but here are some techniques you can try:

1. Get to bed around the same time each evening, and wake up around the same time each morning. This coincides with your body's circadian rhythm.

2. Turn off technology at least sixty minutes prior to closing up shop for the day.

3. Pay attention to sleep cycles. Most of the research I've done here points to the following four sleep cycles:
   a. Sleepiness
   b. Light sleep
   c. Deep sleep
   d. REM/dreaming

   Each of these cycles is ninety minutes, so timing your sleep in a manner which you wake up at the end of one of these intervals helps you feel more rested.

4. Avoid large meals at night. Pigging out close to bedtime activates digestion, which gets in the way of good sleep. Additional good-sleep hacks can be found on the intra-webs.

Exercise. Nutrition. Sleep. Perhaps you're reading this chapter on taking care of your body, and asking yourself the question, "Why?" "Why should I put in the time and effort to get physically fit?" Here are three reasons:

1. **Leadership is difficult.** Leading a business, a church, a team, or a family requires energy over sustained periods of

time. It also demands the ability to make tough decisions. Energy and decisiveness can be directly linked to our level of fitness.

2. **Physical fitness increases our ability to think clearly.** Clarity is one of a leader's best friends. Clear-thinking leadership brings both focus and comfort to the team you lead. It's difficult to follow somebody who lacks focus. It's disconcerting to a team when their boss zig-zags constantly.

3. **A fit body releases you to be more creative and confident.** A well-rounded approach to fitness incorporating exercise, great nutrition, and restful sleep frees you to become a healthier, less-anxious version of yourself. As stated earlier, one of the most influential things you do as a leader is bringing a more-aligned, healthier, and less-anxious version of yourself to the team, business, or church you lead.

I could keep going here, but you get the point. I'm deeply concerned for leaders who are dismissive of the physical fitness component of alignment. Their disdain is to their detriment. "I don't have time, I'm too tired, or I don't like to sweat" are some of the weak excuses we need to kick to the curb.

So, the first two components of personal alignment are spiritual hunger and physical fitness. Growing in these two pursuits produces amazing dividends in your leadership effectiveness. Yet there is still more alignment ground to cover. A third component of personal alignment is psychological integration. We'll dive into the thought processes and emotions making up this critical part of personal alignment in chapter three.

Reflection questions

1. What investments are you currently making in your physical fitness?
2. Which of these three—exercise, nutrition, or sleep—are you neglecting? Why?
3. Who can you invite into your life to hold you accountable in these three areas?

CHAPTER 3

ALIGNMENT COMPONENT 3: PSYCHOLOGICAL INTEGRATION

"Whenever we get unexpectedly knocked over in life, it is whatever is inside of us that spills out" ~ Dr. Paul Meier[1]

Psychological integration brings together the way we think and the way we feel. The better integration between these two, the more aligned we become. The fuller our emotional tank gets. The less integration between our thoughts and emotions, the emptier our tank gets, and the less aligned we become. My experience with the long dark tunnel of major depression many years ago is proof positive of these ideas.

Major depression crashed into my life during a season of great growth in the church we were leading. The church was enjoying its best year of our tenure. We added a second Sunday gathering to accommodate the increased attendance. Giving was up, people were growing spiritually, and finding their fit.

I was married to Laura, the beautiful love of my life. We had four amazing boys. We lived in a nice house with a pool. Externally, everything in life was great. But internally, I was an emotional train wreck.

Intense insomnia, waves of sadness, paralyzing anxiety, and

loss of hope were but a few of my daily realities. I believed—inaccurately—my life was over. The unrelenting emotional pain forced me to the brink of suicide. Dark thoughts controlled me.

I went to a counselor at my wife's request. His first words to me? "John, you need to learn how to be nice to yourself." Wow—powerful stuff. I didn't have a clue about how to be nice to myself back then—especially when it came to my thinking processes. It took practice (and a network of amazing people) over a long period time to get rid of decades of inaccurate thoughts and replace them with truth.

> You can't pour from an empty cup

Somebody has said: "You can't pour from an empty cup." Bringing a full emotional cup to the people you're leading and caring for is one of the most influential things you can do as a leader, now and in the future.

The third component of personal alignment—psychological integration—includes both our thinking processes and our emotions. What we think and feel about God, ourselves, and others determines in many ways the degree of health and fruitfulness we experience in leading our family, team, business, or church.

When clients come to us reporting depression and/or anxiety, we dig into how they're processing life from a thought and emotions perspective. If they report suffering deep wounds from their childhood, we encourage them to see a licensed counselor to work through those issues. Counselors are skilled at scrubbing out deep emotional pain. In many instances, clients use our mentoring service to help process what their counselor is telling them.

Proverbs 19:8 says, "He who gets wisdom loves his own soul." We humans are three-part beings: spirit—the part of us which connects to God; body—the physical house in which our spirit resides; and soul—our thought processes and feelings. Getting aligned psychologically includes positioning our thought processes with truth, and identifying, owning, and properly processing our emotions.

Thoughts are the pieces of information received by our brain. Feelings are how we react to those pieces of information. Behaviors and choices result from what we think and how we emotionally respond to what we think. With these brief explanations in mind, let's take a deeper dive from a biblical perspective on these two powerful pieces of psychological integration.

Thought Processes: Key Scripture Passages

2 Corinthians 10:5 reminds us, "We demolish arguments and every pretension that sets itself up against the knowledge of God, and we take every thought captive and make it obedient to Christ." Let's briefly unpack this verse.

1. *arguments:* The Greek construction here indicates the idea of "accumulated thoughts." It speaks to thoughts which over time have taken up residence in our mind.
2. *every pretension:* A pretension is a thought of human origin preventing us from knowing God accurately. The way we think about God significantly impacts our personal alignment.
3. *every thought:* The idea here in Greek is "thought pattern." Every means every.

Does Paul really imply we are to take every pretension and every thought captive and make them line up with truth? Yes, every last one.

The implication in this Scripture verse is we have the power, if we belong to Christ, to choose what we think about. Mercifully, we don't have to get our thoughts under control by ourselves. We have the help of the Holy Spirit, and hopefully a network of helpful relationships available to us. As we partner with Him in prayer, and invite wise, trustworthy people into our lives, unhealthy thought processes, lies, and pretensions, are often pushed to the surface.

Our job is to take those destructive thoughts and subject them to the truth of God's Word. Whatever thought doesn't line up with the truth ... out it goes. And then we replace the inaccurate thought with an accurate one.

Obviously, this process takes practice. Practice isn't sexy. It's not flashy nor trendy. But in the Gospel of John, chapter 8, Jesus said: "If you *continue* in My teaching, you are really My disciples. Then you will know the truth, and the truth will set you free." Jesus' use of the word "continue" here suggests that applied and practiced truth liberates us! Consequently, the Holy Spirit invites us to practice telling ourselves the truth. He encourages us to subject our thoughts to the integrity of God's Word. Remember, if a thought doesn't line up with His written Word ... out it goes.

Applied and practiced truth liberates us

Ephesians 4:17-24 is another important passage of Scripture dealing with our thought patterns. It says:

> So I tell you this, and insist on it in the Lord, that you must no longer live as the Gentiles do, in the futility of their thinking. They are darkened in their understanding and

separated from the life of God because of the ignorance that is in them due to the hardening of their hearts. Having lost all sensitivity, they have given themselves over to sensuality so as to indulge in every kind of impurity, with a continual lust for more. You however, did not come to know Christ that way . . . You were taught, with regard to your former way of life, to put off your old self, which is being corrupted by its deceitful desires; to be made new in the attitude of your minds; and to put on the new self, created to be like God in true righteousness and holiness.

Let's explore these verses in Ephesians for a moment:

1. "How the Gentiles walk" – In the first half of this passage, Paul described the vicious downward cycle of sinful living: Sinful living starts with—you guessed it—futile thinking. Prolonged futile thinking leads to darkened understanding, ignorance, and hardness of heart. The end result is abandoning all restraint and giving oneself over to destructive desires. This downward pathway starts with our thoughts.

2. Then Paul proceeds to outline what I like to call the "Sanctification Sandwich" in the rest of the passage: First, put off the old man. Second, renew your mind—your thought processes. Out with inaccurate and destructive thinking, and in with the truth. Third, put on the new man. Right in the middle of the process of putting off the old way of life and putting on the new way resides the renewing of our mind.

What we think, and how we feel about what we think, impacts us on every level of life. It affects our personal relationships. It influences our professional life. It flavors our leadership.

Jesus said in Matthew chapter seven: "He who hears these words of Mine and puts them into practice is like a wise man who builds on the rock." If we're serious about getting our thinking aligned and keeping it that way,

> What we think, and how we feel about what we think, impacts us on every level of life

we have to *practice*. Out with the lies, and in with the truth. One of the major contributors to my suicidal depression many years ago was believing lies about myself, about God, and even about other people.

Our Emotions: The Preventive Approach

As I stated at the beginning of this chapter, "You can't pour from an empty cup." So the logical question is, how to do you keep the cup full? How do we top off our emotional tanks? It's my contention we have three tanks as humans: spiritual, physical, and emotional. Behaviors in each of these containers cross over and influence each other. However, each tank requires its own set of behaviors to get and stay full.

I have heard well-meaning Christians say: "If you take care of the spiritual part of your life, you don't need to be concerned about your emotions." To which I respond: "So if I take care of my spirit—the part of me which connects to God—then there's no

> We have an emotional tank that needs tender, loving care

need to pay attention to my body? I can eat whatever I want and be a couch potato with no negative effects on my health?" Of course, they respond, "Well, no." *We have an emotional tank that needs tender, loving care.*

So, how do we take ownership in a preventive manner when it comes to keeping our emotional cup full? The good news is we don't have to understand a complex twelve-step process to gain emotional fullness. We need only to grasp this most important axiom: *Discover what fills up our emotional tank and schedule it into our calendar.* Simple to understand . . . harder to execute.

> Discover what fills up your emotional tank and schedule it into your calendar

For me, time spent in nature fills my emotional tank. We live in a state with beautiful lakes and beaches. One hour staring at the crystal-clear blue waters of Lake Michigan fills my emotional tank. I feel revived, centered, even happy after a sixty-minute session planted on a beach, watching water.

Several years ago, Laura and I had the privilege of taking in the wonders of Glacier National Park in Montana. Around every turn we repeated these words: "Can you believe what we're seeing?" The beauty was beyond our ability to put into words. We stood mesmerized at the beautiful snow-capped mountains, the awe-inspiring waterfalls, and the pristine rivers and lakes within that national gem of a park. One day in Glacier National Park filled up the emotional tank.

Exercise and time spent with friends also fill my emotional tank. We've already discussed exercise in chapter two, and we'll focus on the relational component of personal alignment in chapter four, so no need to elaborate on those two items right here.

What does it for you? What activity, location, hobby, or relationship, fills your emotional cup? Discover it, create space in your calendar to pursue it, and treat those emotional-tank-filling activities with the same degree of care and respect you would an appointment with a client or team member. Remember, you are responsible to care for your emotions. It's your job and nobody else's. Remember the word ownership.

Our Emotions: The Curative Approach

In Mark 4:21-23 Jesus said, "Do you bring in a lamp to put it under a bowl or a bed? Instead, don't you put it on its stand? For whatever is hidden is meant to be disclosed, and whatever is concealed is meant to be brought out into the open. If anyone has ears to hear, let him listen."

For most of my walk with Jesus, I've interpreted His words here as a threat to expose my weaknesses to the world, in order to shame me. In the past several years, I'm seeing this passage of Scripture differently. I think Jesus is teaching this in Mark chapter four: God wants to bring into the light those hidden hurts and wounds that continue to damage us. His intent isn't to embarrass us; it's for us to be healthy and free.

What can you do when your emotions are deeply troubled? How do you navigate life when your feelings are all over the place? How do you cooperate with God in His quest to push into your conscious awareness emotional injuries from the past which are still hurting you in the present?

Much of our discussion in this chapter so far has centered on preventive measures relating to psychological integration. Preventive steps are almost always easier than curative ones—and almost always less expensive.

But what can you do when you feel so stuck emotionally that the curative approach is necessary? How do you care for your feelings when they are troubled? How do you process the emotions of anger, sadness, fear, rejection, anxiety, loneliness, helplessness, inferiority, etc., which threaten your personal alignment?

I want to suggest a practical curative pathway for you. I encourage you to try journaling your way through this process. You will likely need the help of a mentor and a therapist to guide you on this journey. When you find your heart troubled:

1. **Identify your feelings—without judging yourself.** Try to put a name to what you're feeling in the moment. The identification steps go much more smoothly when you avoid telling yourself the following: "I shouldn't feel this way," or "I must be a weakling, or an emotional runt." Be kind to yourself in the identification step. Give yourself some grace. Be your own best friend instead of your own worst critic. Take time to name the emotion(s) you're currently experiencing. I'm not suggesting in this step you be ruled by your emotions. Rather, I'm encouraging you to pay attention to them.

2. **Find a quiet place where you can be alone with your feelings.** Where is your quiet spot? The place where you temporarily get alone with your emotions. Go there and stay put for a while. Open your journal and write down, to the best of your ability, what you're feeling in the moment. I remember a journal entry of mine a while back starting with the words: "Lord, I feel incredibly lonely this morning." Those few words opened up a much lengthier heartfelt prayer written out to God. I left that quiet place with better perspective—dare I say, God's perspective—on what my emotions were doing that morning.

3. **Take responsibility for your emotions.** It's so human to blame others for the way you feel. "If my spouse would just treat me better, I wouldn't be so angry" or "If my boss wasn't such an ogre, I'd be happier" are immature ways to deal with your emotions. Remember the overarching principle of *ownership* outlined in the introduction of this book. As an adult, you and you alone are responsible for your emotions.

   Do other people influence your emotions? Of course, they do. Even so, it's ultimately your responsibility to identify your feelings and then steward them properly. Yes, you'll need the help of God and other people to help you sort things out, but neither God or other people are responsible for your emotional state.

4. **Invite a network into your emotions.** Your emotions find healthier territory in the company of your Heavenly Father and safe, competent, caring people. God understands your emotions better than you do. Asking Him to help is a brilliant move. Safe, competent, and caring people can assist you with gaining perspective on your feelings. Remember your need for a *network*.

   > Nobody thinks accurately in a vacuum

   I've lost count of the times a listening ear of a friend, a mentor, or a counselor helped me accurately frame what I was thinking and/or feeling. If it seems like you're collapsing under the weight of your emotions, it doesn't mean you're weak or less valuable. It means you're human. Let your network help. Here's the truth: *Nobody thinks accurately in a vacuum.* God, plus safe, competent, caring people, counselors, and mentors are a key part of the alignment journey.

I remember several years ago speaking at a church on the subject of emotional health, and after the talk, a thirty-something young lady came up to chat. She took issue with the idea of needing a network to be emotionally healthy. I recall her saying, "I disagree with the idea I need a network to deal with my depression." She was adamant about her position until I posed this simple question, "How long have you been struggling with depression?" Her response was, "Ten years." With as much compassion as possible, I said to her, "I don't think your approach is working. You need a network."

As I draw this chapter to a close, let me pose the "Why" question once more. Why should we work hard at getting aligned psychologically? Why should we expend the effort? What is there to gain?

Our thoughts, and the emotions we attach to them, influence everything in our lives. Our relationships. Our health. Our behaviors and choices. Our leadership. Our thoughts about God, ourselves, and others, and the associated emotions we attach to those thoughts, shape the entire course of our life.

The pieces of information our mind thinks about, and how we respond emotionally to them, impacts the trajectory of our life more than we imagine. I think it's possible to trace back every decision or choice we've made in life to our thoughts, and our feelings about those thoughts.

If we're serious about getting aligned personally, the impact our thoughts and emotions have on our life's direction must compel us to roll up our sleeves and give these two power brokers proper attention. In many ways, how we process these two determine the quality of the life we live. And they most certainly impact the effectiveness of our leadership.

Gaining traction with psychological integration is a major alignment milestone. When you make progress, celebrate! Do the happy dance. But understand, your personal alignment journey is not finished yet. Another critical component is yet to be explored: replenishing relationships. We can work hard at the first three components, but if we ignore relational health, our alignment quest will be disrupted.

Reflection questions

1. Do I have a quiet spot where I can safely process my thoughts and emotions? If not, what can I do to create or find that type of space?
2. Am I taking responsibility for my thoughts and emotions, or am I blaming other people?
3. What is the current status of my relational network? Who within my network is safe to process my thoughts and emotions with?

The pieces of information our mind thinks about, and how we respond emotionally to them, impacts the trajectory of our life more than we imagine

CHAPTER 4

ALIGNMENT COMPONENT 4: REPLENISHING RELATIONSHIPS

"Friendship is born at that moment when one person says to another, 'What! You too? I thought I was the only one.'"
~ *C.S. Lewis*[1]

In Genesis 2:18 God says unequivocally: "It is not good for the man to be alone." He spoke this about Adam, who at the time, enjoyed a perfect relationship with the Heavenly Father. No

> We need both our vertical relationship with God and horizontal relationships with people to be aligned

disruption existed between Adam and his Creator. They walked together in the Garden of Eden regularly. And yet, God saw Adam as needing another human with whom to share his life.

This account from long ago proves something—we need both our vertical relationship with God *and* horizontal relationships with people to be aligned. A for-real relationship with our Heavenly Father and safe, honest, replenishing relationships with people are required to tap into the power of alignment.

I am writing these words in the middle of the COVID-19

pandemic quarantine. Replenishing relationships have taken on a new form—via phone, FaceTime, and Zoom video. While grateful for these forms of connecting, I miss face-to-face, eyeball-to-eyeball communication. Some of our best friends stopped by the other day to chat. Laura and I were on our porch and our friends were on the sidewalk—twelve feet away. Seeing and catching up with them was amazing. But everything inside of me wanted to rush over and hug them.

The pandemic's quarantine has reinforced this truth: We humans require a relational network. The important questions you and I must answer are, who's in our network? Who's missing from our network? Which people can we add to our web of relationships? Here are a few relationships we need in our network:

1. **Spouse** – Your spouse is a vital part of a healthy network, but he or she can't be the only friend in your relational grid. If you're single, maybe a sibling is your closest friend.

2. **Close Friends** – A close friend is a safe, reliable, person you can trust, and somebody who knows everything about you but loves you anyway. If you're male, you need a guy or two who fit this description. If you're female, a girl or two who know you at this level become confidants you can pour out your heart to regularly.

3. **Hangout Friends** – People who make you laugh and give energy to you instead of taking energy from you. Laughter is medicinal. It releases feel-good chemicals in our brain, reducing our stress and lifting our mood. I thank God for the friends in my life who help me loosen up (you know who you are).

4. **Accountability Friends** – These friendships include buddies who pray with you, have permission to challenge you, and aren't afraid to tell you what you need to hear.

5. **Mentors, Coaches, and Counselors** – Mentors, coaches, and counselors are people who help you process life. They come and go depending on the season you find yourself in, but you always need one or more of these three relationships to help you look at life from a clearer perspective.

I think most of us would agree with this idea: *life is so much better when done with people.* Yet parents, team leaders, CEOs, and pastors often find themselves in lonely spots without sufficient other-human support. Why? What is it about leadership that can be so isolating?

Sometimes the problem is philosophical. "You can never have any close friends in the church or business you lead!" This declaration was thrust upon me as a young pastor by more than one seasoned leader. I was a greenhorn, and didn't have enough experience or confidence to push back on their opinionated position. Coming out of college, where friendships were many and rich, the thought of having no close friends in the church I was serving made me sad, anxious, and confused.

Life is so much better when done with people

Today, I'm pretty sure most of those cautionary tales issued from hurtful experiences suffered by these leaders. The idea that "you can't have any close friends in the church or business or team you lead" isn't a biblical thought. When you study the life of Paul, you notice he had friends in the churches he served. In the book of Romans, chapter sixteen, he used phrases like "Epenetus, my dear friend . . ." and ". . . Stachys my dear friend . . ." Jesus said in John chapter 15 to the twelve guys following him: "I call you friends . . ." We'll talk in more detail about Jesus' words on friendship later in this chapter.

> The idea "you can't have any close friends in the church or business or team you lead" isn't a biblical thought

So this idea of having no friends in the organization or team you lead isn't really rooted in Scripture. Yet loneliness continues to plague a significant number of leaders. Pastors, for example, are often isolated. A 2017 book from Barna Group, *The State of Pastors*, written from a study of 14,000 Protestant lead pastors in the United States, revealed only thirty-four percent of these leaders reported deep friendships.[2] Do the math—sixty-six percent of these leaders have no deep friendships. That is both a stunning and unacceptable number. Every week, I hear similar stories of struggles with loneliness from leaders. Leadership responsibility has the uncanny capacity to isolate us.

> 66% percent of lead pastors have no deep friendships

Pastors aren't the only lonely leaders. CEOs and managers also report a significant degree of loneliness. I've had management responsibility in the marketplace, and experienced seasons where, due to making tough personnel calls, I felt alone.

In the business world the terminology often used to propagate the idea of leadership isolation is *professional distance*. Be cordial and warm, but keep your distance. Professional distance makes a lot of sense from a legal perspective, especially when it comes to relationships at work between men and women. But it's hard to get away from this fact: *Leadership is highly relational.* If the people I lead feel cared for, appreciated, and sense I possess genuine interest in their lives, they enjoy work more, they grow, and they produce at a higher level. Their level of work engagement soars. They find joy in their role.

> Leadership is highly relational

Please note one boundary always needing to be enforced: if you as a leader feel romantically attracted to a person at work, back off. Keeping professional distance in this scenario makes sense for a lot of reasons.

The question is: Can leaders have close friends in the organizations they serve? I think the answer is yes. Is it advisable? It depends on who you ask. If we polled one hundred leaders, it probably would be a 50/50 split. Each side would tell you either horror stories of getting burned or wonderful stories of rewarding friendships in the organization or team they lead. But I'm choosing to land on the "yes" side of leaders having friends at work, as long as friendship doesn't cloud their ability to make personnel decisions.

Is there risk with friendship? Yes. But *every* relationship carries some degree of risk. I would argue that isolating ourselves carries risk as well—maybe even more. *God has wired you and me for deep friendship.*

> Our purpose in life is intertwined with people

Our purpose in life is intertwined with people. That doesn't change when you become a leader. I don't think we will get where God wants us to go as leaders if we choose to live in a relational desert.

So, fear of what *could* go wrong keeps many leaders in a friendship wilderness. But fear isn't the only dynamic getting in the way of friendship for leaders. *Busyness* also presents a thick barrier. I've never seen pastors, business executives, and team leaders busier than today. Our discretionary time seems at an all-time low. The very thought of carving out time to nurture friendships throws some of us into an anxiety attack. And yet ironically, healthy friendship is often the exact antidote for our anxiety.

As I stated earlier in this chapter, the world is dealing with a pandemic called COVID-19. In the state I live, we are currently in a restrictive lockdown. For a stretch of two months, I was unable to be in the same room with our children, daughters-in-law, or our grandbabies. No face-to-face moments with dear friends. I know others have it worse than me, but it doesn't negate the real sense of isolation I felt. *Personal alignment is impossible to achieve in a relational vacuum.* And the repercussions of isolation can cause serious misalignment.

In 2018, we sadly saw high profile cases of suicide, including Kate Spade, Anthony Bourdain, and Andrew Stocklein, a 30-year old pastor who left behind a wife, three young children, and an evangelical megachurch in California. In 2019, Jarrid Wilson, a California church leader, author, and mental health advocate, died by suicide at age 30. Most recently, Darrin Patrick, a pastor and friend to pastors, died from an apparent self-inflicted gunshot wound. As gut-wrenching as these tragedies are, they're only the tip of a much bigger iceberg.

> Personal alignment is impossible to achieve in a relational vacuum

According to the Substance Abuse and Mental Health Services Administration, in 2017 there were more than 47,000 completed suicides in the United States.[3] Experts believe the real number of completed suicides is closer to 190,000. It's reported there are six attempts for every completed suicide. If their math is correct, it means over one million suicide attempts occurred in 2017 in the United States.

So much of the suicide epidemic can be traced to a single root issue—*loneliness*. In the Gospel of John, chapter 15, verse 15, Jesus said to the twelve men following Him, "I no longer call you servants, because a servant does not know his master's business. Instead, I have called you friends, for everything that I learned from My Father I have made known to you."

The word translated "servant" here means literally, "bond-servant." Jesus told the guys closest to Him: "I no longer call you bond-servants, instead I call you friends . . ." His words represented a huge shift. Jesus established a new relational platform with these men. It would be marked by unrestrained friendship. He would keep nothing from them. Friendship from Jesus' perspective implies openness and availability.

These twelve dudes were still His followers. He was still their Teacher and Master, but moving forward He would relate to them differently—He would treat them like intimate, familiar friends.

In today's world, doesn't it feel like we're growing increasingly isolated? We're more connected technologically but seemingly less connected relationally. Many of us are comfortable living our lives publicly on social media but feel increasingly uncomfortable talking face-to-face with people.

I've already told you about my intense battle with suicidal depression many years ago. My struggle is fully detailed in one of my other books, *Unshakable You: 5 Choices of Emotionally Healthy People*. It was the darkest season of my life. I would have never made it through the long dark tunnel of major depression without the love/support of my wife and three couples who came alongside me, loved me, prayed for me, and laughed with me. *Friendship is an irreplaceable part of personal alignment.*

Conceptually, most of us buy into the idea of friendships being important. It's the living-it-out piece we struggle with. The question is, why do we struggle with it so much? What gets in the way of a leader and friendship? There are too many barriers to explore in this book, but here are three major obstacles:

1. **Fear**
   a. The fear of rejection. We fear being found out. I think we're often afraid (especially us men) of being found fraudulent. We're terrified people will discover we're not as together as we project ourselves to be. And when they do discover the real us, we fear they will reject us.
   b. The fear of getting burned. For some of us, friendship suffers because we fear getting hurt again. If you've been wounded relationally, I'm not minimizing your pain. Staying away from certain people is understandable, and in some cases advisable. The apostle Paul told his young apprentice Timothy to avoid Alexander the metalworker who had done Paul a great deal of harm.

   I devote an entire chapter in my book, *Unshakable You: 5 Choices of Emotionally Healthy People,* to the subject of protecting yourself from people who intentionally want to hurt you. Jerky people see life through a negative prism. They are experts at criticizing you, but refuse to lift a finger to help you improve. You always feel worse about yourself when around them. Whatever you do is never good enough. Your sense of worth takes a beating. They are simply awful to be near. Avoid these types of people like the plague! But the truth is, every relationship in our life carries the ability to hurt us at some level. All relationships possess some degree of risk. However, as my friends in business used to tell me, "No risk . . . no reward."

2. **Social Media** – I use Facebook, Twitter, and Instagram. I'm not against using social media, but the social platforms possess the capacity to fool us. They can trick us into thinking we're experiencing friendship when we're actually not. Digital friendships alone are not enough to keep us aligned. In fact, social media posts can make other people's lives seem better than they really are, which can get in the way of friendship too. Then there is a third hurdle hindering our friendships.

3. **Calendar** – Busyness wars against friendship. Consequently, here is an all-important question for us to consider: *What can we let go of today that creates space for friendship?* I served in the corporate world for twenty years. I understand the demands the marketplace can put on our schedules. I also pastored for sixteen years. Church life can wreak havoc on your calendar. Seasons of being incredibly busy exist in both worlds. The problem is, busy seasons have the uncanny capacity to expand and become our only season.

> What can we let go of today that creates space for friendship?

We can get overscheduled to the point where our friendships get squeezed out. One day you wake up, and realize you haven't spent any quality time with friends in weeks (or months). Again, prolonged disconnection from your relational network is not healthy for your soul. One friend of mine pointed out that isolation can be your only choice sometimes for a short season. Agreed . . . just don't allow it to become a way of life.

It's important to understand isolation is not the same thing as solitude. Solitude has purpose behind it. Time spent alone with God, moments of reflecting and thinking, and minutes focused on recalibrating are good uses of solitude. Even then, solitude is good only in small doses. Extended solitude can lead to isolation, and isolation is the devil's playground. Depression and anxiety thrive when we are relationally detached. These evil twins thrive under the cover of secrecy. Depression and anxiety diminish when exposed to the light of community.

> Depression and anxiety diminish when exposed to the light of community

Leader friends, can I challenge you to have a heart-to-heart conversation with Father God and figure out the real reasons your calendar is so jammed? Is it fear? Is it the limited benefit of social media? Is it busyness? Is it fear of what you'll discover about yourself when you slow down?

At this point, perhaps you are thinking: "John, why should I care about friendship? I've gotten this far without friends!" A leader several years ago actually said those exact words to me. I felt both sorry and afraid for him. Let me give you two huge reasons you should care:

1. **Replenishing friendships significantly impact our personal alignment.** They keep our emotional tanks full. Good friends celebrate victories with us, and help bear our burdens. *A shared win is multiplied. A shared burden is automatically cut in half.* The depth of our friendships plays an irreplaceable role in our personal alignment.

   As I researched for this book, I came across study after study trumpeting the impact of good friendships on our lifespan. One reason researchers think friendships and health are linked is because nourishing friendships help our body process stress. Friendships help us flourish. Another reason you should care about this subject?

   > A shared win is multiplied. A shared burden is automatically cut in half

2. **Healthy friendships keep us safe.** They help us stop lying to ourselves. Nourishing friendships protect us from the devil's diabolical plan to paint us into a relational corner and then take us out. My wife and those loyal, loving friends I spoke of earlier kept me safe while making it back from the brink of suicide twenty-eight years ago.

   We need a thriving relationship with God and wholesome relationships with people to get and stay aligned. We must have people we can vent to, friends we can laugh with, and companions who will hold us accountable. A mentor, coach, or counselor can help us process the emotions or thought patterns that keep troubling us. These relationships foster personal alignment.

Even in light of the overwhelming evidence regarding the positive emotional impact of friendships, and their proven ability to keep us aligned and safe, perhaps you're still protesting on the inside: "I know friendships are important, but I don't know how to make friends." Ah, I have help for you still. Real quickly, let me give you seven hacks or shortcuts to help you get started with building healthy friendships:

Hack 1: Go First

Rather than waiting for people to reach out to you, be brave and take the first step. You may need to try several times before determining the other person's level of interest. Friendship-building starts with intentionality on our part. Dale Carnegie wrote: "You can make more friends in two months by becoming interested in other people than you can in two years by trying to get other people interested in you."[4]

Hack 2: Be Reciprocal

Adult relationships that aren't reciprocal are unhealthy. In a thriving friendship, sometimes you're doing the encouraging and the listening. Other times you're receiving the encouragement and being listened to. One-sided friendships usually don't flourish.

Hack 3: Be Kind

Kindness is relational currency. It puts change in your friendship pockets you can draw out when needed. We live in an increasingly unkind world—kindness will set you apart. It will make you a friend-magnet. Kindness is in rare supply in our culture—and desperately needed.

Hack 4: Grow Your Listening Skills

For leaders, listening can be difficult. We tend to talk a lot. I remember my seventh-grade teacher yelling at me in exasperation one day: "Shut up, John! All you do is talk, talk, talk!" She was amazingly prophetic—I talk for a living. Fortunately, paying attention to others is a skill that can be developed. It starts with listening to understand rather than to reload. Appropriate eye contact, welcoming body language, and reflective listening communicate interest. If you're easily distracted, work hard to stay focused on what your friend is sharing with you.

Hack 5: Be Trustworthy

As we've already mentioned, broken trust from past relationships paralyzes some leaders. So being trustworthy will make you stand out. The ability to maintain confidentiality, to be reliable, and dependable are foundational to healthy relationships. Do what you say you're going to do. If you want a potential friend to trust you—be trustworthy.

Hack 6: Be Wisely Transparent

Again, here is where many leaders jump off the friendship boat. Fear of being known in a deep way gives them the willies. So, behave wisely here. Be transparent in bite-sized chunks. The more trust grows, the more you can share about yourself. Often, we either open up too soon, or we never open up at all. Both extremes are unhealthy. Becoming wisely transparent deepens relationships.

I think it's important to briefly distinguish between appropriate transparency, and inappropriate transparency. The apostle Paul, one of the greatest Jesus-followers of all time, wrote to his friends in Rome: "So I find this law at work: Although I want to do good, evil is right there with me." *Wait . . . what?* Did Paul just tell the entire world about his wrestling match with the flesh?

Paul was a godly man and an amazing leader. But he understood something about himself—he hadn't arrived. Notice he didn't go into graphic detail about his struggle. He didn't air all of his dirty laundry to the entire crowd. Nor did he pretend he was perfect. He simply acknowledged reality: "I'm still growing in grace. I haven't figured it all out yet. But with the help of God I'm making progress."

Understanding and admitting we're imperfect leaders in need of God's grace, leading a group of imperfect people in need of the same grace, helps us move toward healthy transparency. Eventually and hopefully, you'll locate a couple of friends of the same gender who you can tell your deepest, darkest secrets to. But not every person in your life should have that level of access to you.

Hack 7: Be Available

Busy leaders be advised: friendship rarely—probably never—happens accidentally. It almost always results from purposeful planning and action. Therefore, do everything possible to gain some margin in your life. Create space on your calendar for friendship.

It's unlikely we'll handle the multiple pressures of leadership in a healthy way if we try to do it alone. *You and I need friends.* Godly friends. Wise friends. Truth-telling friends. Committed friends. Funny friends. The simple act of telling a confidant about the pressure you feel reduces the weight, simply because it's shared. And when your friend responds with a kind word, the load may not actually be lighter, but it feels lighter. Sharing the load doesn't make it disappear—it just makes it easier to bear.

You and I will not reach healthy alignment without investing heavily in friendship. Leadership calls out our deep need for honest, meaningful, and replenishing relationships. When you come to your ultimate demise, your life will be measured not by the size of the church or business you lead, nor how high on the leadership ladder you've climbed. It will be measured in large part by the friendships you've nurtured. You won't be remembered for your accomplishments as much as you'll be remembered for the relational value you've deposited in people. So, let's put away fear, make room in our calendars, and dive into the rewarding world of relationships.

Our alignment journey is nearing its destination. Spiritual hunger, physical fitness, the integration of our thoughts and emotions; and replenishing relationships set us up to lead impactfully. But one more component is needed for our alignment to be rock-solid and unshakable: life-giving rhythms. Chapter five will unpack a few of the most important rhythms we need to discover and implement to get and stay aligned.

Reflection Questions

1. What gets in your way of prioritizing friendship?
2. In what ways would your leadership life improve if you increased the amount of time spent with friends who bring out the best in you?
3. Who is mentoring you? Who are you mentoring?

CHAPTER 5

ALIGNMENT COMPONENT 5: LIFE GIVING RHYTHMS

"If you study the rhythm of life on this planet, you will find that everything moves in perfect symphony with everything else— by grand divine design." ~ Suzy Kassem[1]

Great leaders cultivate great rhythms. The healthier your rhythms, the more aligned you become. The more aligned you are, the better your leadership.

Rhythms can be boring to the untrained eye. Not many leadership books exist that focus on the power of tempo and cadence. But here's the truth: Great leaders have developed great rhythms. The most successful people in the world have tapped into their power.

Great leaders cultivate great rhythms

Pablo Casals, the world's foremost cellist was once asked why he continued to practice four-to-five hours per day. Casals answered: "Because I think I'm making progress." Casals understood the impact of rhythm.

I have several friends who suffer with Atrial Fibrillation or

AFib. With AFib, the heart's upper chambers (atria) beat out of coordination with the lower chambers (ventricles). Another word used to describe AFib is arrythmia.

Arrhythmia is a problem with the rate or rhythm of your heartbeat. It means your heart beats too quickly, too slowly, or with an irregular pattern. Many factors can affect your heart's rhythm, such as having had a heart attack, smoking, congenital heart defect, and stress. Some substances or medicines may also cause arrhythmia. Symptoms of arrhythmia include: fast or slow heart beat; skipping beats; lightheadedness or dizziness; chest pain; shortness of breath, etc.

My purpose in this chapter is not to educate you about AFib. Rather, it's to talk with you about a major truth AFib illustrates:

The longer our life is out of rhythm, the higher our risk is of breaking down.

I've lost count of the number of good people who've done incredibly stupid things simply because they were exhausted. Extended fatigue lowered their defenses, and they made choices which were totally out of character for them. Things which are out of rhythm are unhealthy.

The longer our life is out of rhythm,
the higher our risk is of breaking down

Here are several examples of rhythms:

1. **Work/rest rhythms** – daily, weekly, quarterly, and annually. The bulk of this chapter focuses on the work/rest rhythm.

2. **Spiritual rhythms** – In chapter one, we explored the power of daily moments of meaningful connection with God. The singular pursuit of God needs to have times of gathering with like-minded believers added to it in order for us to be aligned and healthy. When it comes to our relationship with Jesus Christ, none of us is an island.

3. **Physical rhythms** – exercise, sleep, and good nutrition. We discussed these in chapter two. We can better serve the people we lead when we're physically fit.

4. **Relational rhythms** – In chapter four, we unpacked the relational component of personal alignment. We advocated for nurturing those relationships that fill up our emotional bucket. However, it's healthy to mix in times of solitude, much like Jesus modeled for us. Jesus had the relational rhythm figured out. He moved seamlessly between large crowds, the twelve disciples, and having time alone.

Solitude in small chunks is usually healthy. Solitude in large chunks is not. Solitude is different than isolation. Solitude usually has purpose to it. For example, thinking, reflection, and listening for God's voice. Isolation is different. It often lacks purpose. We tend to fall into isolation as opposed to intentionally choosing it.

Like it or not, leading a company, team, or church sets you up for relational isolation. It sounds weird, because as a leader you're always around people. But being *around* people and being connected to people are two different things. Giving energy to people and receiving it from people have different impacts.

When was the last time you spent an hour or two with good friends having no agenda other than to laugh and have fun? If you can't remember, beware. Your relational rhythm is likely out of whack.

You and I were created by God for friendship. In fact, by ourselves, we won't reach our full leadership potential. But at the same time—we need alone time too. Time for introspection and reflection. Thinking time. Listening time. Moments where it's just us and Father God.

As stated earlier, the bulk of this chapter focuses on our work/rest rhythm. How we behave when it comes to the interaction between work and rest impacts our alignment significantly. Way too often, leaders who are passionate about their work throw caution to the wind in terms of their schedule. And before long, they wind up misaligned from a calendar perspective. Work becomes more difficult, fatigue sets in, and because they're not well-rested, leaders can find themselves not enjoying their calling as much as they used to. Figuring out and implementing a sustainable schedule helps you keep aligned, energetic, and healthy.

If you're a leader, God hasn't called you to a sprint—He's called you to a marathon. Marathoners run at a different pace than sprinters. Usain Bolt set a world speed record of 27.8 miles per hour during the 100-meter sprint in the 2009 World Championship. Dennis Kimmetto set the world record for the marathon in 2013. What do you think Dennis' average pace was? Thirteen miles per hour. Marathoners run at a different pace than sprinters. You won't finish the leadership marathon God has called you to if you're always sprinting. Incidentally, working at a sustainable pace as a long-term strategy affords you the capacity to sprint in those moments you need to.

Personal alignment calls for a healthy work/rest rhythm. The longer this rhythm is out of sync, the higher our risk of breaking down. If our physical heart is out of rhythm, it creates a host of collateral issues with our health. An out-of-sync gear spinning incorrectly in an engine can shut down the whole apparatus. Things out of rhythm long-term don't work at full capacity.

A while back, Laura and I spent a week vacationing in Florida. We took in Venice Beach on a windy day, and the waves were impressive to look at. The never-ending ebb and flow of the surf mesmerized me. In some ways, I think ocean waves are one of God's creative messages to us about a healthy work/rest rhythm. Push onshore and then retreat offshore. Flow and then ebb. Work hard on the right things. Then rest. Short bursts of energy, followed by moments of recess.

With those Venice Beach waves in mind, allow me to quickly outline four sub-rhythms of a work/rest rhythm that help you get and stay aligned: These work patterns are so practical you'll probably say "Well, duh," after each one. But remember: What you know matters. What you do with what you know matters more.

Four Work/Rest Sub-Rhythms

1. Daily

In Genesis chapter 1, when God was creating the universe, we observe a repeated sequence at the end of each creation segment. "And there was evening and then there was morning." This sequence speaks to stopping and starting points.

A daily rhythm has to do to with knowing when it's time to start and stop work each day. Most leaders have no trouble starting their work day. They tend to struggle with stopping. After so many hours of work in a given day (for most people, this is eight-ten hours), you get tired. Welcome to humanity. Daily rhythms will be somewhat different for all of us, but research tells us that for most of us normal humans, after eight work hours in a day, our productivity falls off a cliff. When you're tired after a solid day of work, accept it as a God-given stop-signal. Give yourself permission to clock out. *I'm not calling you to laziness—I'm calling you to sensibility.* Laziness and workaholism are evil twins that weaken your long-term impact. "And there was evening, and then there was morning."

> When you're tired after a solid day of work, accept it as a God-given stop-signal

2. Weekly rhythm

Another name for the weekly rhythm is "Sabbath." You've probably heard the term more than once. It's interesting to read Exodus 34:21, where God commanded the Israelites to observe Sabbath rest, even during times of "plowing and harvest": "Six days you shall labor, but on the seventh day you shall rest; even during the plowing season and harvest you must rest."

For a farmer, plowing and harvest seasons are the busiest times of the year. Yet even in those stretches, God made it clear rest wasn't a luxury—it was an essential. In other words, when a busy season is on the horizon, we don't get a pass. We're commanded to deliberately make

> Sabbath is a gift from God, reminding us every week our life's calling belongs to Him, not to us

room in our weekly schedule for a day of rest, relaxation, and renewal. We're to treat these appointments with the same degree of care and commitment we would give to an appointment with a teammate or a client.

> It's a short leap from workaholism to arrogance

This second rhythm means taking a real day off each week. After completing the work of creation, God rested on the seventh day. He didn't rest due to exhaustion. He rested to set an example for us ambitious humanoids.

A weekly day off serves as a reset button. It's a gift from God, reminding us *every* week that our life's calling belongs to Him, not to us. Practicing Sabbath rest reminds us God is our source and provider. It requires us to believe God is still at work, even when we aren't.

Here's a scary thought:

It's a short leap from workaholism to arrogance.

Pushing the reset button every week reminds us our work ultimately is God's, not ours. A weekly day off helps us remember we're not indispensable. It keeps us from becoming full of ourselves. When we regularly blow by His command to rest weekly, it's easy to start taking credit for results. The apostle Paul offers a different view: "I planted, Apollos watered, but God gave the increase" (1 Corinthians 3:6). One major benefit of a weekly Sabbath is the resetting of this perspective.

Now . . . does our week blow up sometimes and we miss a day off? Yes. But if most or all of our weeks explode and we keep missing our day off, something is broken about the way we approach work. We're setting an unsustainable pace, we will find ourselves out of rhythm, and eventually face emotional trouble. In the end, our leadership will be negatively impacted.

Multiple studies completed by organizations such as Proctor & Gamble, the National Association of Manufacturers, and the National Association of Electrical Contractors prove the genius of a forty-hour work week. Here's the short version of these studies: Each organization took a group of workers from the same team, and for two months, one group worked sixty-seventy-hours per week, and the other group worked forty hours per week.

At the end of two months, the sixty-seventy-hour per week group didn't out-produce the forty-hour per week group. Shocked? So were these organizations. As they dug deeper into the results, they learned several things. The workers in the forty-hour group were fresher in the morning. They got down to business right away and put in a solid eight hours. Their colleagues in the sixty-seventy-hour per week group took longer to get started in the morning. They made more mistakes. They were sick more often than the forty-hour per week group.

I wonder how much we would concentrate at work if we knew we only had forty hours to complete our tasks and no more? We would waste less time and apply more focus for sure. Again, I'm not lobbying for a specific number of hours each week, I'm lobbying for us to be honest with ourselves. The results of these studies should give every leader pause. I'm not telling you how many hours to work every week. I'm telling you that after forty, your productivity starts to rapidly decline. And it's not just the number of hours we work; often it's what constitutes those hours. Forty hours of wall-to-wall high-energy events will have the same impact on your health as sixty hours of less intensive work. Some of you reading this chapter have blown by this weekly rhythm of Sabbath for so long, you may have forgotten how to take a day off. Here are a few helpful tips:

- Go easy on technology. It's so tempting to glance at work email on your day off. Put the phone far away and use it sparingly. Allow voicemail or even airplane mode to be your friend. Keep the PC shut.
- Carve out time for regular exercise. See chapter two for more details on getting your body moving.
- Engage in emotional tank-filling activities. A drive along one of the Great Lakes' shorelines clears my mind and rejuvenates my emotions.
- Spend time with replenishing friends.
- If you're married, take your spouse on a date.

These first two sub-rhythms—daily and weekly—are foundational. If we ignore them, the next two rhythms won't help us as much.

3. **Quarterly rhythm**
   Every ninety days, get out of your zip code and take a day away for relaxation, reflection, recreation, and rest. This quarterly respite will refresh you. At my last job in the corporate world, I enjoyed five weeks of vacation annually. I would take a week off every ninety days, and two weeks off in the summer. I would return from these quarterly breaks energized and ready to produce. You may not have the luxury of five weeks off, but every ninety days, a change of scenery will help you get and stay aligned.

Every ninety days, get out of your zip code

---

4. Annual rhythm

Ah vacation . . . a real vacation. What does one of those look like? I've observed many leaders who struggle to really be on vacation even when they do take one. The line between work and their personal life seems blurrier than ever. During the COVID-19 pandemic, with most leaders working from home, the line has been obliterated for many.

A getaway where you're answering emails, taking calls, or catching up on some work—is not a real vacation.   Disconnecting from work for a vacation is not wasted time or selfish

> Disconnecting from work for a vacation is not wasted time or selfish behavior

behavior. It's a crucial part of maintaining a healthy work/rest rhythm in the face of the ever-present demands of our leadership calling.

So, there you have it. Physical rhythms. Spiritual rhythms. Relational rhythms. Work/rest rhythms. Why does achieving these healthy rhythms matter?

Let me share three incredibly important reasons why we need to pursue and implement life-giving rhythms:

1. **Jesus lived His life in a beautiful tempo of work and rest.**
    A perfect rhythm of relationships and solitude. Time praying alone with His Father, and time praying with the

twelve disciples as a group. If we're His followers, then it makes sense to follow His example here. Jesus was the most-aligned leader in human history—and consequently, the most impactful leader ever.

2. **You won't escape the negative consequences of arrhythmia for long.**
A lack of rhythm will catch up to you. Fatigue, anxiety, and depression will knock

> Jesus lived His life in a beautiful tempo of work & rest

on your door, often suddenly, when you consistently live on the edge of exhaustion. Additionally, you are much more susceptible to doing incredibly stupid things when you're fried. You don't want sleep-deprived electrical workers repairing power lines, nor bleary-eyed doctors performing surgery, right? Then why do you think it's okay to lead from a posture of exhaustion? When you lead tired, you hurt yourself, and the family, team, business, or church you serve. And you put yourself in an incredibly vulnerable position. Your defenses are lowered when you are chronically bushed.

3. **Healthy rhythms prepare you for success.**
Getting yourself to the next level *before* the family, team, company, or church you lead gets to its next level prepares you to withstand the strain inherent in the next level of those organizational units. Remember, the most impactful thing you can do to help the family, team, company, or church you lead is to bring a healthier, more aligned, less anxious version of yourself to the party.

In Matthew 11:28-30, Jesus extended an invitation to every leader: "Come to me, all you who are weary and burdened, and I will give you rest. Take my yoke upon you and learn from me, for I am gentle and humble in heart, and you will find rest for your souls. For my yoke is easy and my burden is light."

When you watch Jesus in the Gospels, you discover He was never stressed out, except for a brief moment in the Garden of Gethsemane. He never appeared to be in a hurry. How did He pull that off? Here's how:

Jesus only did what He saw His Father doing, and only said what He heard His Father saying (John 5:19). Nothing more, nothing less. And yet, He was incredibly successful. He finished His race. He led impeccably. If Jesus is our model, if He's the one we're following, why are we so stressed? I think a major reason is our lack of rhythm. Perhaps we've taken on more responsibility than He's asked us to.

Here's the challenge for leaders: the notion of a "9-to-5" work schedule is unrelatable. If you're leading an organization, work doesn't come at you in an eight-hour per day, five-day per week stretch. It comes at you like ocean waves. Times of onshore flow approach you at different speeds and varying volumes.

The waves of leadership action are challenging to regulate. If a leader is inattentive, his or her life can be all onshore flow with very little accommodation for offshore retreat. For some, their work life is all flow, and no ebb, except when they collapse into bed each night, exhausted once again from a lack of healthy work/rest rhythm. Months and months of unrelenting work with little-to-no down time sets the trap for anxiety, burnout, and depression. If any of these three enemies crash into your life, you will be forced to "ebb"—and likely for longer than you want.

One more big challenge with rhythms is knowing when you're out of rhythm—especially when you are a newcomer to the alignment journey. How do you know if you're out of whack from a rhythm perspective? Is it even possible to know? Yes, it's possible.

Four Signs You Might Be Out of Rhythm:

1. **Sunday Evening Dread**
   If you feel a knot in your gut on Sunday night as Monday approaches, one of the reasons might be that you're out of rhythm. (Yes, it could mean other things, like you dislike your job, or have an ornery team, etc.) But if you love what you do, and the looming week feels like a gauntlet you need to just get through . . . you may have a rhythm problem. Pay attention to those feelings of dread. They are informational. Those emotions may be revealing your work flow and ebb are out of rhythm.

2. **Increased Irritability**
   I used to think irritability was always a sign of immaturity. And while it often is, sometimes irritability can be linked to a lack of rhythm. If your work life is all flow with no ebb, no matter how much you love what you do, irritability won't be far behind. Feelings of irritation can be a God-given signal that the wave-action in your life is out of kilter.
   Maybe your heightened irritability is the result of encountering a string of emotionally-draining events with little-to-no-time-in-between for recuperation. Consider it a possible indicator you're overcommitting time and emotional resources. You may be all flow with little-to-no ebb.

3. Endless Physical Ailments

If you're encountering a string of illnesses—respiratory problems, flu, sinus infections, migraine headaches—of course these could be due to solely physical sources. But I wonder how often their source is elongated stress due to schedule-arrhythmia?

I recall on numerous occasions, when my work life was out of rhythm, I would get sick during vacation. It happened like clockwork. My boys would complain, "Dad you always get sick on vacation." It was disappointing to them, because I wasn't my usual fun self when ill.

Does sickness visit you more often than not? If so, it's possible you're out of rhythm.

4. Discomfort with Downtime

If you get fidgety when not working, uncomfortable with taking a breather, and don't know what to do with yourself during downtime, I can almost guarantee you're out of rhythm. God didn't create you to be the Energizer Bunny during all your waking hours. He's given you ocean waves as a creative reminder to work diligently, but to rest just as purposefully. Work should include short bursts of productive effort, followed by short seasons of retreat. Watch the ocean waves, and you'll soon discover God's rhythm to help you get aligned.

If downtime makes you crazy, you may be running on adrenaline and cortisol. Adrenaline increases your heart rate, elevates your blood pressure, and boosts your energy supply. It is a hormone released from the adrenal glands and its major action, together with noradrenaline, is to prepare the body for "fight or flight." Cortisol, the primary stress hormone, helps regulate blood pressure and cardiovascular function.

The long-term activation of the stress-response system and the overexposure to cortisol and other stress hormones that follows can disrupt almost all of your body's processes. This puts you at increased risk of many health problems, including anxiety and depression.

> Work resulting in proper outcomes is a gift from God. *Workaholism and laziness are perversions of that gift*

Work resulting in proper outcomes is a gift from God. *Workaholism and laziness are perversions of that gift*. They interrupt the wave action God has designed us to flow with. If you're all flow, watch out. Soon you won't be crashing onto a beach—you'll be crashing into a wall. If you're all ebb, be wary. You're wasting time and talent, both of which God will hold you accountable for.

Here are two of my favorite Scripture passages regarding work:

- "The Lord God took the man and put him in the Garden of Eden to work it and take care of it" (Genesis 2:15).
- "Whatever you do, work at it with all your heart, as working for the Lord, not for men, since you know that you will receive an inheritance from the Lord as a reward. It is the Lord Christ you are serving" (Colossians 3:23-24).

So, my leader friend—get to the beach. Watch and listen to the waves. Let the genius of God's creation speak to you about a healthier approach to work and rest. And then commit to following His simple but brilliant plan for your alignment and longevity.

Reflection Questions

1. What has been disrupting your work/rest rhythms?
2. What positive steps can you take to remedy those disruptions?
3. Who can you be accountable to regarding your work pace?

EPILOGUE

MY LEADERSHIP WISH FOR YOU

"Beginning well is a momentary thing; finishing well is a lifelong thing." ~ Ravi Zacharias[1]

Wow! It's hard to believe our brief alignment journey has come to an end. Thanks for allowing me to spend time with you. After reading about these five alignment components, you might be wondering: "John, these five pieces are so basic, do they really work?"

I would respond, "of course they do!" But let some of our clients answer the question instead. When leaders come to us for help, they're often struggling with fatigue, anxiety and/or depression. Some are even considering quitting vocational ministry, or leaving their business, or team. Others, tragically, are thinking about abandoning their marriage. When we take them on this five-step alignment journey, almost always, somewhere along the way, they experience a significant breakthrough.

Check out these unsolicited comments from our clients.

"I'm dreaming again."

"My creativity has returned."

"My confidence is back."

"I feel the clouds dissipating and the light shining once more."

"I'm energized for the first time in months."

"I'm leading better than I have in a long time."

"I'm sleeping better than ever before."

These results happen over and over again during the alignment process. *It's a simple, yet amazingly powerful journey.*

As I close out *Unshakable Leader*, I find my heart full of wishes for both your personal and professional life. Let me share three:

Wish 1: Get/Stay Aligned

> Remember why you signed up to lead in the first place: love for God

Remember why you signed up to lead in the first place: love for God. At some level, you've obeyed His direction to lead your family, business, team, or church. Make time spent with Him your priority. Create space for meaningful times of connection with God on a daily basis.

Keep filling your emotional and physical tanks as well. Nobody else will do it for you. Remember the word ownership. Keep your life packed with replenishing relationships. Remember the idea of a network. Take time to laugh, love, exercise, and rest. Obey the Sabbath. Get six-to-eight hours of sleep per night. Remember the power of *rhythms.*

Getting/staying aligned in your personal world enhances your professional world. It extends your leadership shelf-life. A better-aligned version of yourself causes leading a church, company, team, or family to become more fulfilling and impactful. Plus, you'll have more fun along the way. I've included in the Additional Resources Section a link to our personal alignment checklist. This free resource will provide a quick read on your current level of personal alignment.

Wish 2: Get/Stay Focused

Remember your calling . . . your assignment . . . your mission . . . your vision. Keep these four building blocks in view. Allow them to serve as a filter for what you will and won't do. Every day, try to do at least one thing which moves the ball down the field of those four leadership cornerstones. As much as possible, work in your areas of gifting and passion.

> One of the more important opportunities you enjoy as a leader is identifying the God-given greatness in people and calling it out of them

Refuse to allow the invisible pull of the ~~~ out the macro. Spend more time t planning; and less time reacting, fir tasks you can and should delegate. disruptive moments will always be pa as a leader. Just don't let disruption be

Share the leadership load. Refuse to to sit on the sidelines applauding while of the more important opportunities you enjoy as a leader is identifying the God-given greatness in people and calling it out of them. One of my home church's core values is, "Everything is better in teams." Indeed.

Wish 3: Get/Stay Centered

Remember what really matters. If you've surrendered control of your life to Jesus, you are a son or daughter of Father God. *Everything else good in your life is gravy.* Remind yourself often: The most important disciples in your life live under your own roof. Work on your marriage. Spend time with your children. Go to their soccer games, dance recitals, and karate demonstrations. Teach them how to love Jesus.

> The most important disciples in your life live under your own roof

Work *from* your identity, not *for* your identity. Your identity, if you belong to Christ, is that of an adopted son or daughter. Paul tells us in Galatians chapter four we are even more than adopted sons and daughters of our Heavenly Father . . . we also enjoy the status of being heirs. Stay centered on who you are in Jesus Christ.

My prayer is you would take the five alignment components— spiritual hunger, physical fitness, psychological integration, replenishing relationships, and life-giving rhythms—and imbed them deeply into your personal life.

The better aligned you are, the healthier you'll become. The ____ier you get, the more likely it is you will reach your full ____. You will become an unshakable leader. Those you lead ____ greatly. You will lead better, longer, and enjoy it more. ____day when the vast majority of leaders are aligned, their leadership load is shared, and they can do what they love for the long haul. I envision a tomorrow where leaders prize their marriage and children as their most important accomplishments. I see an era where leaders enjoy deep, replenishing, and fulfilling friendships.

My wishes for you are tied to the Great Commission: "Therefore go and make disciples of all nations…" In our families, our teams, our organizations, we'll fail Jesus' imperative if we don't get/stay aligned, focused, and centered. But if we do—we'll become unshakable leaders—and our families, our teams, our businesses, and our churches will become the unstoppable forces God has always meant them to be.

I hope you choose to become an unshakable leader.

I'm rooting and praying for you!

John

ACKNOWLEDGMENTS

Writing a book is a team effort. It only comes to life by the combined force of many talented and inspirational people. God has graciously given me a team possessing both talent and the ability to inspire.

First of all, thank you to my wife, Laura. Your words, "John it's time for you to write another book" were the catalyst for this project. You are my best friend, and a true gift from God.

A special shout out to my sons Aaron, Andrew, Nathan, and Chad, and my daughters-in-love Anna, Amanda, and Klar. I love each one of you deeply, and value your friendship.

Much gratitude to Janet Blakely for your expert assistance with editing the manuscript. Your keen eye and way with words continue to amaze me.

Thanks also to Keigh Cox for lending your graphic art and layout skills to the project. You are a pleasure to work alongside.

Many thanks to the Converge Coaching team—Jamie, Jim, Mary, and Jaime. I couldn't ask for better teammates. You are talented, high-character people who do great work, lighten my load, and make me laugh.

Last, but certainly not least, I am grateful to God for His faithfulness. In good times and bad, in seasons of chaos and peace, He is the unchanging Rock. I'm forever grateful He took an angry, unhappy, and empty teenager and breathed His life into me. "He will cover you with His feathers, and under His wings you will find refuge; His **faithfulness** will be your shield and rampart" (Psalm 91:4).

NOTES

Introduction
1. Barna Group, *The State of Pastors*, 2017, www.barna.com
2. Harvard Business Review, *"What Makes Entrepreneurs Burn Out,"* April 10, 2018 by Eva de Mol, Jeff Pollack, and Violet T. Ho, https://hbr.org/2018/04/what-makes-entrepreneurs-burn-out/.

Chapter 2
1. Jim Rohn, Quote by Jim Rohn, America's Foremost Business Philosopher, reprinted with permission from SUCCESS. As a world-renowned author and success expert, Jim Rohn touched millions of lives during his 46-year career as a motivational speaker and messenger of positive life change. For more information on Jim and his popular personal achievement resources or to subscribe to the weekly Jim Rohn Newsletter, visit www.JimRohn.com or www.SUCCESS.com.
2. Jimmy Dodd, *Survive or Thrive: Six Relationships Every Pastor Needs*, David C. Cook, 2015.

Chapter 3
1. Dr. Paul Meier, *Be Strong and Surrender: A 30-Day Recovery Guide*, 2016, Dvorak.

Chapter 4

1. C.S. Lewis, *The Collected Letters of C.S. Lewis,* Harper Collins, 2017.
2. Barna Group, *The State of Pastors,* 2017, www.barna.com.
3. Substance Abuse and Mental Health Association, www.samhsa.gov.
4. Dale Carnegie, *How to Win Friends and Influence People,* Simon & Schuster, 1936.

Chapter 5

1. Suzy Kassem, *Rise Up and Salute the Sun,* Awakened Press, 2011.

Epilogue

1. Ravi Zacharias, *I, Isaac, Take Thee, Rebekah,* W Publishing Group, 2004.

ABOUT THE AUTHOR

John Opalewski graduated from Oral Roberts University and served as a pastor for 16 years. He is a certified Coach with Natural Church Development (NCD). He has served as an associate pastor, campus pastor, and lead pastor. For 20 years, John also worked in the Information Technology industry.

John's experience as a leader in both the church and business arenas has made him a sought-after international speaker, consultant, and mentor. He and his wife, Laura, have been married more than 30 years and have four sons, three daughters-in-law, and three granddaughters.

Laura and John founded Converge Coaching, LLC in 2012 to help leaders lead better, lead longer, and enjoy it more.

CONTACT AND ORDERING INFORMATION

Additional books are available for purchase through John's website: www.convergecoach.com

Bulk discounts available

eBook platforms are also available:
Amazon Kindle
Barnes & Noble (Nook)
iBookstore
Sony
Kobo
Copia
Gardners
Baker & Taylor
eBookPie

For more information about other resources and services available through Converge Coaching, LLC, please visit our website: www.convergecoach.com

Contact John at: john@convergecoach.com

ADDITIONAL RESOURCES FROM CONVERGE COACHING

Personal Alignment Checklist

Here is a quick checklist that can help determine your level of personal alignment: https://convergecoach.com/resources-new/

Unshakable You
5 Choices of
Emotionally Healthy People

John Opalewski

Emotional health is sometimes elusive. We often run our lives on fumes, dangling on the edge of burnout or depression. Difficult relationships, overcommitted schedules, traumatic events, or the gnawing sense we're unlovable—all will drain our energy.

What can you do? If you're burnt out or depressed, how do you get healthy? If you're healthy, how do you stay that way? You start by making five choices. *Unshakable You: 5 Choices of Emotionally Healthy People*, introduces key behaviors which move a depressed person toward recovery, and keep an emotionally fit person well.

Pick up a copy today at www.convergecoach.com
E-book available on iPad, Kindle, Nook, Kobo, Copia and many other platforms

Putting the GOOD in GOODBYE
A Healthy Conversation About the
Comings and Goings of Church People

John Opalewski and Jim Wiegand

Every pastor faces the pain of people leaving their church. Sleepless nights, deepening doubts, and anxiety about the future often accompany each future.

Leader, how can you stay healthy and on mission when the reality of mobility among churchgoers punches you in the face? You start with yourself.

Putting the GOOD in GOODBYE: A Healthy Conversation About the Comings and Goings of Church People, introduces five key behaviors which keep a leader steady in the face of members walking out the door.

Pick up a copy today at www.convergecoach.com

Pastor Disaster
***Confronting the Growing Crisis
among Church Leaders***

John Opalewski

Pastoring a church can be hazardous to a leader's health. Difficult people, dysfunctional families, unrealistic expectations, and spiritual warfare present challenges to a pastor's longevity and health. More than 1,000 pastors leave the ministry every month due to burnout, contention in their church, or moral failure. Their exodus has contributed to the decline of the Church's impact on Western culture.

The question is . . . what can we do? How can leaders lead longer and better? This practical guide, written for pastors, leaders, and churchgoers, identifies the real problems behind the current leadership crisis. It provides workable solutions to strengthen leaders and help the Church re-establish its influence.

Pick up a copy today at www.convergecoach.com
E-book available on iPad, Kindle, Nook, Kobo, Copia and many other platforms